URBAN EVERESTING

Mark Cramer

for Martha, my wife and partner in calculated risk

First edition ISBN: 978-1-950255-04-7

First published by Wordbound Media LLC, 2019

URBAN EVERESTING

Paris

CONTENTS

MINIMALIST INTRODUCTION: WHAT FOR?   6

THE LAST HIKING FRONTIER: RIGHT OUTSIDE YOUR   9
DOOR

WHAT IS A GOOD URBAN HIKE?   13

EVEREST POINT SYSTEM   17

MORE ON EVERESTING: SAN FRANCISCO VS. SEATTLE   24
(and PITTSBURGH)

CLOSING IN ON EVEREST   28

LARGEST URBAN FORESTS   30

MOST PUBLIC STAIRWAYS   34

IDEAL ENDINGS: SPRAWL-FREE ACCESS TO   40
WILDERNESS OR RURAL LANDSCAPES

HIGH LINES   44

THE BEST CITIES FOR HIKING: RANKING   46

SAFETY TIPS   52

CASE HISTORY: EVERESTING IN LA PAZ   54

WHAT IF I LIVE IN A FLAT CITY?   70

MINIMALIST INTRODUCTION: WHAT FOR?

Hermann Hesse's Narcissus and Goldmund may be the ultimate trekking novel. It is the wanderer's struggle to find himself. The detachment of being on the road, on foot, is not an escape from the horrors of existence but an attempt to define his coexistence with the pestilence of his time. We go out in the mountains, but then we come back.

From the get-go, Henry David Thoreau was also aware that returning from the woods was unavoidable.

In school we were led to believe that Thoreau's Walden was an attempt to abandon modern life as a recluse. But from the "Economy" section of Walden we learn that his two years in the woods were but an experiment in how to simplify life in the face of a world based on accumulation.

We were told that the Walden experiment had been a failure because Thoreau came back to the town. But his time in the woods was more a question of finding the right balance and his walks in the woods continued beyond Walden, as an expression of freedom.

"If a man walks in the woods for love of them half of each day, he is in danger of being regarded as a loafer; but if he spends his whole day as a speculator, shearing off those woods and making earth bald before her time, he is esteemed, an industrious and enterprising citizen."

– Henry David Thoreau, *Life Without Principle*

In his essay "Walking" we learn that the time spent sauntering is freedom we extract from a system in which we cannot be totally free. "Our expeditions are but tours, and come round again at evening to the old hearth-side from which we set out. Half the walk is but retracing our steps."

Like Thoreau, Ivan Illich assures us that when we are on our own two feet, we express our freedom from an unequal system.

> *"People on their feet are more or less equal."*
>
> – Ivan Illich, *Energy and Equity*

He adds, "Beyond a certain speed, motorized vehicles create remoteness which they alone can shrink. They create distances for all and shrink them for only a few."

For some of us, urban hiking is one way to extract freedom from a deterministic environment. It is a passive-aggressive confrontation, like blades of grass slowly but surely cutting through a crack in the side-walk.

Paris

La Paz

THE LAST HIKING FRONTIER: RIGHT OUTSIDE THE DOOR

Urban hiking is so obvious that we cannot see it. We are blinded by a perception that views human creations, such as the Brooklyn Bridge, as separate from nature. The American emigration from compact towns to sprawling suburbs was, in part, a conditioned yearning to be closer to "Nature."

Nature was sold as the separation of residence from commerce. Suburbanites became tethered to their cars even for simple errands. A trade was made whereby residents were able to see more "green" space around them, in exchange for filling this space with motor vehicles, electric cables, plumbing infrastructure and manicured lawns. In departing from a walkable downtown, suburbanites evolved from bipeds to voluntary quadriplegics, vastly expanding carbon emissions, power grids and waistlines.

The obscene quantities of water required to sustain unnatural green lawns had never been required by the prairies that such lawns sentimentally caricature.

The suburban and exurban illusion of wide-open spaces really means longer distances in motorized vehicles to perform simple duties like buying a loaf of bread or picking up a child from school. Is it closer to nature to use less human energy in order to perform daily errands?

This call of the wild did not only spring from sentimentalism. It was aggressively promoted by lobbies from the automotive, tire and oil industries, through massive flows of feel-good, in-your-car, on-your-lawn propaganda, fueling some municipalities to uproot successful light rail systems. Convivial store fronts and local hangouts once reached on foot became an endangered species.

The ideology of the great escape from civilization has extended to the realm of travel, where hiking, trekking and mountain climbing are presented as a form of purity that would contrast with daily life that is tainted by cement, steel, plastic, noise and congestion. But even Mount Everest, the ultimate exurb of the tourism circuit, is now littered with oxygen canisters, sundry gear and an occasional dead body.

Our pleasure for walking and hiking seems to derive from a synchronicity between the natural movement of our bodies and the natural contours we follow. But why restrict natural contours to prairies, mountains, forests, rivers and hills? Why not include rugged urban environments as well?

We humans are part of the animal world and what we build, with materials derived directly or indirectly from the earth, remains a part of nature, sometimes in healthy equilibrium and other times in unsustainable conflict with the earth that spawned them.

What we construct is to serve our natural needs for survival, shelter, comfort, warmth and conviviality. Just how different in original purpose is this from beavers building dams, birds meticulously crafting a nest or ants gathering in work crews to build hills and tunnels and even raising livestock: in their case, aphids? Does the bird nest take away from the naturalness of the tree? Does a high-rise anthill demean the floor of the rainforest?

> *"Beavers dam streams, which can cause a dramatic change in the surrounding ecosystem, in order to build a den and a place to raise their young. It is interesting that this change is viewed as natural, even though it is changing the environment to suit their needs, but clearing an area of land by humans to build a house is viewed as destructive and unnatural even though it may be done for the same purpose."*
>
> – Roger Stone, "Humans as a part of nature," *http://web.colby.edu/humanslashnature/2015/09/20/humans-as-a-part-of-nature/*

Thoreau might agree that our conflict with the earth we are part of begins when we exceed our Epicurean needs and make possessive demands: the difference between drinking coca tea and producing cocaine.

Does the crow perched on the electric wire perceive that this resting place is less natural than the branch of a tree? If you believe that humans are not animals, then the crow appropriating the power line has engaged in an affront against humanity, the natural empire striking back.

As an integral part of nature, we humans have always interacted with our geography. We can do so mindfully or we can do it stupidly. Both options have existed in the human history of place.

It is precisely when we assume ourselves to be above and beyond nature that we injure and scar the geography we depend on. Eventually, beachfront condominiums in Southern California and big-box high-rise hotels on the Costa Brava in Catalunya will not survive. Years, decades or centuries later, the Earth will strike back and punish us for our arrogance, with mudslides, heat waves, droughts, floods, and in one possible scenario, the planet will cleanse itself of its human inhabitants and new species will have a chance to get it right.

One day we might decide to help our geography as a partner. Using materials from the earth, we might decide to dynamite a blight-producing freeway cloverleaf and return the rubble to its source. This is not far-fetched. In cities like Portland, Oregon and Paris, France, riverfront freeways were returned to their pedestrian stewards.

For the most part, the premise of urban hiking is that we recognize our flawed existence to be part of nature. Even the most pristine parts of the earth have been affected in some way by human intervention. A hike across a disappearing permafrost is no "purer" than one that crosses the Brooklyn Bridge.

Some crows have deposited nuts on the street surface so they can be cracked opened by a natural phenomenon: a passing car. Once we agree with the crows that we are a part of nature, a whole new realm of hiking becomes available. In the next chapter we will define urban hiking.

La Paz

WHAT IS A GOOD URBAN HIKE?

Urban hiking is neither an extreme sport nor a walk in the park. It's a mindful physical challenge that will not land you a place in the Guinness Book of Records. It provides many of the health and spiritual benefits of exercise but it can be both fun and educational.

You can call it a sport but it's non-competitive, except, perhaps, with one's own mental and physical limits.

It represents an alternative to the neurotic need for speed so exquisitely explained in Illich's Energy and Equity, long before the accelerated, Google-clicking shrinking of our attention spans.

It is an outdoor sport that embraces geography but it does not require the
latest equipment or designer sport wear, so it provides a respite from consumerism, and with zero carbon emissions. And just because you begin each hike from home or an Airbnb rather than a campsite does not make you a wimp. Measured in cosmic time, your home is no more permanent than a one-night campsite. In the best of urban hiking, your rented or mortgaged living space becomes your base camp.

Urban hiking is multi-disciplinary, at once covering social ecology, urban aesthetics, geology, botany and philosophy, as well as the hiker's own biology.

Three propositions can begin to define the best places for urban hiking:

> ✓ 1. There must be a geographic or physical challenge, as opposed to window shopping on Fifth Avenue. This proposition favors cities with rugged terrain. The presence of numerous public stairways, for example, is one indicator of a good place for an urban hike. When a real forest is located within municipal limits, the city gets extra hiking points. Being able to reach authentic mountains on foot or by public transportation is a major indicator.

✓ There must be sites within the urban or suburban context that are set apart and unique, worthy of being called a destination. Any place where tourist buses cannot get to is a potential urban hiking destination. Some possible destinations: ecological sanctuaries, historic shrines, panoramic lookouts so removed that you cannot hear the traffic below, or a one-of-a-kind restaurant where filling up your human fuel tank becomes a quiet festival.

✓ Ideally, there would be a way out of the city that directly connects with wilderness or rural territory. This escape must be accessible on foot, by bicycle or with a short ride on public transportation that gets you past the sprawl.

In other words, urban hiking is favored by cities that have rugged terrain, hidden surprises and authentic city limits. One of the great thrills of urban hiking is that hikers can forge "new" trails and then draw their own maps! It's a new frontier that may even be close to home. The following chapters will highlight the best urban hiking venues in the USA and around the world, as we designate measurable criteria in order to award the cities their hiking medals.

Urban hiking is more hedonistic than other painfully stoic forms of hiking and climbing. It's easier to stop for a beer or an almond croissant along the way, and after a day's hike, you can return to a base camp with a warm shower. Nevertheless, the hiking cities featured in this dissertation provide settings for big challenges, sometimes with seductive extremes, and like Hesse's Goldmund, along the way you'll make discoveries about yourself.

Author passing on the wonders of human energy to grandson in a climb of 1,125 steps in Laguna Beach, California. The so-called "Thousand Steps" is actually only 225, but these partners did 5 round trips, with fitness freaks and gasping first-time climbers both sharing the mythical seaside stairway.

Hong Kong

EVEREST POINT SYSTEM

Evaluation System.

One note on the evaluation system in subsequent pages. Two criteria did not need ranking. The category "offers unique destinations" is satisfied by all the chosen cities: no need to make comparative measurements. Ditto for "trailheads reachable by public transportation," a prerequisite, since what they call "active transportation" is the ecological partner of the urban hiker.

Finally, if you think your city should have received a Hiking Gold Medal and it doesn't even appear here, send us an angry message with documentation and we'll probably include it in the next edition.

Or if, sadly, your city has been correctly excluded, you can remain there and fight to make your home turf a walkable place. At this very moment around the world, municipal leaders are planning for and building seductive hiking trails, with the help of artists, landscape architects and committed citizens who find great pleasure in getting around on human energy.

It is possible for a relatively flat city to qualify as a best hiking city but urbanscapes with rugged terrain have an advantage. Here's how my Everest Point System works. In cycling there's an extreme sport called everesting, in which the cyclist repeats the same climb-descent until he or she has scaled the height of Mount Everest. It makes even more sense to apply everesting to hiking.

We'll explain the system in both meters and feet for your convenience. Mount Everest is 8,848 meters /29,029 feet high. A climber starts by taking a short plane ride from Kathmandu, Nepal to the Lukla airport, at 2,860 meters / 9,380 feet. There's a 10-day hike to get to the base camp at 5,400 m / 17,700 ft.

The total number of meters/feet climbed from Lukla to the top of Everest is 5,988 meters / 19,649 feet. For purposes of awarding hiking cities with Everest Points, we will round off these total climbs to 6,000 meters / 20,000 feet.

Purists will disparage us for rewarding Everest points to some sea-level cities that offer a full breath of oxygen, that do not require technical equipment for climbing and that treat the hiker to warm showers. However, we refuse to be ashamed to include cities whose air is richer in oxygen than the oxygen-depleted air of the Himalayas.

As for rewarding Everest points, climbs that take place at or near sea level will receive only one ▲   On the other hand, high-altitude cities where you only take in half the amount of oxygen-per-breath that you'd get at sea level will receive ▲▲

A sea-level city with an extraordinary number of nearby mountains may also merit the double-mountain rating.

Hong Kong

Hong Kong

As an example, seven of the walkable peaks in Hong Kong: Sunset Peak (869m), Lantau Peak (934m), Tai Mo Shan (957m), Sharp Peak (468m), Lion Rock Peak (495m), High Junk Peak (344m) and Victoria Peak (554m) total 4621 meters in altitude. In order to reach the 6,000-meter Everest score, you could reclimb some of these peaks on alternate trails, climb other available peaks or scale urban staircases, counting 5 stair steps per meter of altitude.

Hong Kong

Tai Mo Shan on foot or by bike.

Much of the 957m ascent of Tai Mo Shan is paved road, with conveniently placed water faucets. Avid cyclists enjoy this challenge, as well. Awesome panoramic views of city below, the Tai Po Valley and surrounding mountains! There's a weather radar station at the summit, explaining the need for the paved road. If you're considering gaining your Everest points by bike, beware that the average gradient is 9.6% and the entire trip is 9 km. How about the bike-walk variation, whereby you alternate between pedaling and pushing? That's a complete exercise. Have your brakes checked before doing the trip so that you can enjoy the thrilling descent without the nagging fear that your brakes will slip and skip from overheating.

Hong Kong has at least four other major hiking trails, but even if it didn't, its mountains alone offer enough alternatives to achieve a 6,000-meter Everest score.

Hong Kong

Taipei

Taipei, Taiwan is another Everest qualifier with at least a dozen climbs whose starting point is within reach by public transportation.

Qixing Mountain.

The highest is Qixing Mountain, at 1,120 m (3,675 ft). Stair climbers will delight that early segments of the climb are over a rough stone staircase through a narrow corridor of lush vegetation. Careful with your ankles. Near the top there's a chalky stone giving off volcanic gases. Partway down one can complete the descent via bus, if you can handle the hairpin turns in an enclosed vehicle.

Combining Qixing with other climbs, all distinct, including Teapot Mountain, the dramatic Ping Xi Crags and The Four Beasts (4 peaks in one), you can reach the 6,000-meter Everest qualification. Taipei also has more gradual nature trails, such as Zhi Shen Yan Trail, leading to a beautiful temple, as well as a stunning National Forest (see next section), so it would be hard to not reach the 6,000 Everest meters just by doing daily hikes from your urban base camp.

Cape Town

Cape Town, South Africa offers hikes of up to a 1,087m / 3,566ft rise in altitude (Table Mountain), and combining 10 different hikes , including Devil's Peak (1,000m / 3,281ft), you can easily accumulate the 6,000m Everest points and along the way, be treated to awesome panoramic views of the sea, the city, nearby peaks and, from Tygerberg Nature Reserve, a view of Robben Island, the unwanted, long-term residence of Nelson Mandela. Each hike has its own idiosyncrasies. For example, to get to the top of Skeleten Gorge, you need to scale ladders.

Table Mountain.

The impressive views of the ocean begin from the get-go. Parts of the climb have an ankle-threatening staircase of crooked and jagged rocks where every step requires concentration. After 15 minutes there are narrow ledges where the hiker needs to use both hands for support. Here and there are a few shady ledges for a break from the direct sun and slashing winds. You may get hit by big drops in temperature at higher portions. At some segments of the climb of Table Mountain there's a possible return via cable car, if it's in service.

For reasons of both safety and security, you should NOT do Table Mountain alone, and before trying it, enjoy some of the easier climbs to acclimate. By no means should you take a selfie at the edge of the rocky Table Mountain climb or you will not live long enough to regret it, as one unfortunate hiker discovered.

These three coastal cities are all generous with oxygen for the climber. I reserve the more demanding higher-altitude cities for later sections.

Grenoble or Annecy, dueling cities in the Alps, France

My wife and I once did four days of splendid hiking in the Vercors mountains and since then I've searched for the best city as base camp to the Vercors. Grenoble is it. On the other hand, we also hiked from a smaller and more post-card picturesque city of Annecy, climbing the steep Mont Veyrier, 540 m / 1,770 ft, with no need for equipment. Once to the top, we looked straight down upon a magical view of the immense blue alpine lake and city, and straight across to shining glaciers. We paid a price on the steep descent, using muscles that we did not use on the way up and getting sore legs. The canal city of Annecy has a City Hall and active street life, but alas, with a population of only about 55,000, I'd be forcing it to rank Annecy as urban hiking.

On the other hand, Grenoble's population exceeds 160,000 and is considered the capital of the Alps. More peaks are accessible from Grenoble than from Annecy. If you hang out in Grenoble, you won't have trouble accumulating Everest points. Start with a hike from the center of town to the Bastille fortress, 476 meters, with a belvedere overseeing the city and the snow-covered Alps in the distance. You can descend in a bubble-shaped cable car called Les Boules.

Next two days, also from the city center, follow up Bastille with climbs of Mont Jalla (635 meters) and Mont Rachais (1046 meters). On your fourth day in town, take Transisère Bus 5110 from Grenoble to the main bus station of Saint Nizier (40-minute ride) and do the Moucherotte Trail, 9.26 km, total ascent 769 meters, not technically challenging but requires plenty of exertion, rewarded at the top with a 360-degree view that includes Grenoble, the Vercors and Mont Blanc.

So, in four days, you've accumulated nearly 3,000 Everest points. That's already half an Everest. No wonder the Grenoble Tourism Office writes: "Don't be surprised if you come across hikers with boots on their feet and a full pack on their back in the city center. They're not lost or crazy, they're probably just on their way to the Bastille to start their hike."

Starting right from downtown, 820 kilometers of marked trails stretch towards various ranges, including the Vercors. According to Forbes Magazine, 2013, Grenoble was the fifth most innovative city in the world in linking business with ecology, and ranked by the French Association of Paralyzed Individuals as number one city in France. I'm sure we're not the first in giving Grenoble a Gold Medal for hiking innovation.

San Francisco

EVERESTING: SAN FRANCISCO VS. SEATTLE (and PITTSBURGH)

How to evaluate San Francisco and Seattle for potential Everest points? Both have lots of hills, both have public transportation to get to them and both have nearly 100 public staircases. The presence of a stairway suggests that a street may be too steep to climb. (We'll focus on the public-staircases ranking factor in a later section.)

Number of hills: San Francisco 43, Seattle 11

Number of climbs above 100 meters: SF 31, Seattle 7

Gradients: Seattle's highest gradient is 26% (East Roy Street) while San Francisco has 4 climbs steeper than 26%, with Filbert Street at 22nd attaining a 31.5% gradient.

Pittsburgh parenthesis: Pittsburgh has the highest urban gradients, with 4 hills above 26%, the steepest being Canton Avenue at 37%. Such extreme gradients explain why Pittsburgh outdoes SF and Seattle in numbers of public stairways. Once a jazz neighborhood, Pittsburgh's hill district was subjected to urban renewal. The hill where George Benson grew up was leveled to make way for a stadium. But Pittsburgh's hills remain distinctly ungentrified when compared to those of San Francisco and Seattle.

As for access to climbs via public transportation, both San Francisco and Seattle have fine public transportation, with Seattle planning bold improvements. But in 2017, San Francisco outranked Seattle as the number 1 city in the USA for living without a car, by a real estate survey (*www.redfin.com/blog/2017/02/the-best-cities-for-living-without-a-car.html*).

The urban hiker has it easier surviving on foot in San Francisco than in Seattle and this is partly due to a more comprehensive public transport system.

According to the census, in 2016 54.4% of New Yorkers lived without a car, 29.9% in San Francisco, 29.5% in Philadelphia, 23.5% in Pittsburgh and 17.1% in Seattle. Tougher to survive without a car in Seattle, but still possible.

In comparing San Francisco and Seattle, on factors like number of hills, number of hills above 100m, number of gradients above 26% and facility for reaching hikes on public transportation, when all is said and done, San Francisco offers better probabilities for accumulating Everest points. (This is a numerical but not an aesthetic evaluation.) If numbers crunching is at all an indicator, San Francisco is a better place for extreme hiking while Seattle looks superior for cycling.

San Francisco

Everest within reach! Remember that the Everest climber does 6,000 meters. Surely the San Francisco climber, without the aid of Sherpas, can climb all 31 hills of over 100 meters /328 feet. This will total 4,592 meters. The conservative climber can make four of these climbs per day, so the 4,592 meters can be attained within 8 days. (Climbers whose biggest scare is the cost of temporary housing in a SF "base camp," will be motivated to do more than four of these climbs per day. A thousand meters per day is not far-fetched.)

To complete the remaining 1,408, you can choose to re-climb those hills with the best panoramic views at the top, or better yet, those hills that have the best pastry stops. Or, you can climb the remaining 12 hills and/or add a few magnificent stairway climbs.

Approximately 5 stair steps equal one meter in altitude. In the stair climbing section I'll explain how I arrived at that figure. For completing the final 1,408 Everest meters, using 5 steps per meter, you can start with the Filbert East Stairway of 383 stair steps, the equivalent of 76+ meters. Next, try the 16th Avenue tiled stairs, 163 steps: nearly 33 meters.

Combining the remaining hills with staircases, you will have climbed your Everest in San Francisco, with

1. No expensive equipment needed;

2. The opportunity to stop for a calorie-adding glass of beer along the way, and

3. A base camp that, even at SF real estate costs, is cheaper that the Everest base camp!

San Francisco

PS. Don't miss Land's End, part of the Coastal Trail, with a 260-footclimb from rough beach cove to the trail, with a view of the Golden Gate Bridge.

San Francisco

CLOSING IN ON EVEREST

The highest point on the earth, as measured from the earth's center is NOT Mount Everest. The earth is not a perfect sphere and is a bit thicker at the equator due to centrifugal force created by the planet's constant rotation.

According to the National Oceanic and Atmospheric Administration (US Department of Commerce), "because of this, the highest point above Earth's center is the peak of Ecuador's Mount Chimborazo, located just one degree south of the Equator where Earth's bulge is greatest. The summit of Chimborazo is 20,564 feet above sea level. However, due to the Earth's bulge, the summit of Chimborazo is over 6,800 feet farther from the center of the Earth than Everest's peak. That makes Chimborazo the closest point on Earth to the stars." (See: *oceanservice.noaa.gov/facts/highestpoint.html*)

Quito, Ecuador

I was once in Quito during the rainy season and was advised by my hosts that the mountains would be too treacherous for safe climbing and that I'd get plenty of great exercise scaling the numerous hills within the city. I was able to do a number of urban climbs, including a nearly 200-meter-high hill within the city called El Panecillo.

At an elevation of 2,850 meters / 9,350 feet, where the earth's bulge is greatest, Quito is the second highest capital city, after La Paz, Bolivia. The center of Quito is a World Heritage Site, with the least-altered and best-preserved historic centers in the Americas.

The Ruca Pichincha hike, is technically within the city of Quito. The public transport that takes you to the trailhead at 3,945 meters /12,943 feet is the TeleferiQo. From there the path takes you upward to 4,698 meters / 15,413 feet, for a climb of 753 meters. At this altitude, where each breath gives only half the oxygen you'd get at sea level, 753 meters is considerably more strenuous than the plus 1,000 meter climbs in Hong Kong, Taipei and Rio de Janeiro (next section).

From the top of Ruca Pichincha, on a relatively clear day, you can see the city spreading out below like a colorful quilt.

Try another hike within the city: the expansive Parque Metropolitano in the northern, Batan Alto neighborhood. The marked trails include a 6.21-mile (10-kilometer) route with many side trails, and views from the park that include the volcanoes Cotopaxi, Cotacachi, Cayambe, and Antisana. This hike gets rave reviews from visitors.

Ups and downs in Quito take many forms. There is one climb that merits a public urban staircase (see later chapter) LLLL for Quito: climbing the Basilica including one of its twin towers, for a 360-degree view of the city and surrounding mountains. For a $2 ticket you can do this 45-minute climb, part stair steps and part ladders. No American insurance company would insure this church climb of 115 meters / 375 feet. Blogger Anil Polat tells us not to look down nor to become discouraged by people who preferred to quit halfway up. (*https:// foxnomad.com/2010/06/03/the-path-to-the-top-of-quitos-la-basilica-church-in-pictures/*)

So, how to classify Quito in the scheme of Everest points? What if we did the Ruca Pichincha without the cable car? That would be 1,475 m / 4,839 ft, a quarter of an Everest.

Blogger Mattie Quigley has done Ruca Pichincha without taking the TeleferiQo? Quigley writes: "Years ago this was said to be dangerous with both robberies and assaults. However, it is now a somewhat common training ground for Ecuadorian trail runners. I've summited this over a dozen times and never had any problems. However, do be wary of the dogs about 20 minutes into the hike. They can get slightly aggressive though I've never been bitten." Quigley notes: "lack of preparation can become dire as the mountain can quickly go from a sunny clear day to   completely enveloped in fog. Many hikers believe they have finished at the base of the rock but the hike is still about an hour or two from its end. Past the cave, the trail becomes much more difficult to follow and some false trails have led many hikers astray." (*https://www.summitpost.org/rucu-pichincha-without-the-teleferico-and-more/1018822*)

LARGEST URBAN FORESTS

Rio de Janeiro

Tijuca Forest, Rio de Janeiro (see "World's Largest Urban Forest was Planted by Hand," Stephen Messenger, *Tree Hugger* (22 August 2010). From bottom to top, the climb is 1022 m (3353 ft). Hiking this trail is only medium difficulty but requires endurance. The good news is that it's largely a shaded trail with waterfalls. The Tijuca Forest was mainly planted by hand. The land had been stripped of its trees because of development. In 1860 the emperor Pedro II ordered the terrain replanted with the native species that used to thrive along Brazil's coast.

Thanks largely to trails in and around this immense forest, Rio de Janeiro qualifies by Everest criteria. If you do this hike plus nine other recommended hikes, and throw in the 215 steps of the urban staircase wonder, the Selaron mosaic staircase, you reach the 6,000-meter equivalent of an Everest climb.

Taipei City

A national park within city limits, Yangmingshan National Park is a 114-sq-km rainforest ecosystem, between 200m and 1,200m above sea level with a wide range of habitats for animals and plants, and more than 150 types of butterflies. Tijuca Forest only has 92 square kilometers but is universally ranked above Yangmingshan probably because the Taipei national park is not all forest.

A number of US cities can be proud of their own urban forests. In "The 10 Best US Cities for Urban Forests," Wendy Koch, *USA Today* (5 Feb 2013) notes that "…a federally funded survey looked at the 50 most populous U.S. cities to see which have the most parkland per capita as well as which do the most to create green spaces and make them accessible to the public.

The survey was done by American Forests, a non-profit group that restores and protects forests. The top ten, unranked, in alphabetical order, are: **Austin, Charlotte, Denver, Milwaukee, Minneapolis, New York City, Portland (Oregon), Sacramento, Seattle** and **Washington, D.C.**

Portland, Oregon

Of these, Portland, Oregon's Forest Park is the largest city forest in the lower 48 states, and three times the size of Paris' sprawling Vincennes Forest. Forest Park boasts at least eight distinct hiking trails, including Ridge Trail, with a 340 m / 1,116 ft variation in altitude. Not quite enough to earn Everest points in a few outings, but if you hike creatively and regularly, you can eventually equal an Everest. Outside of Forest Park, Portland offers numerous other hikes within the city limits, including the Sauvie Island wildlife area in the Columbia River.

"It's totally possible to spend every weekend in the woods without even getting a driver's license," according to Allie Donahue ("The Best Portland-Area Hiking Trails Accessible by Public Transportation," *Willamette Week*, July 7, 2015).

Only a mile from the Southwest 5th Avenue bus mall, for example, is Council Crest, with an 820-foot elevation gain, the highest point within Portland city limits. From the top, a view of five Cascade Range mountains. Don't miss the extinct volcano, Mt. Tabor, with attractive stair climbing.

Vancouver, British Columbia, Canada

One of the weirdest climbs in the world is found right here, with access by shuttle. It's Grouse Grind, a climb of "only" 1.8 miles with a gain in elevation of 853 meters / 2,800 feet. So why is this strange? First, many segments of the climb are on stairs, treacherous irregular steps, a total of 2,830 stair steps in all! Some do this as a fitness exercise and time themselves, while others just want the reward of the Douglas fir forest view at the top, along with a cold beer at the balcony restaurant. Second, it's a one-way-only hike. You have to pay for a cable car to get back down.

In order to gain Everest points, there are other climbs near the city. For example, Crown Mountain, also accessible via public transport, with a summit of 1,504 meters, where making it to the top requires managing steep trails with some exposed segments where one could slip on moist rocks or be belted off a ledge by the wind.

Then there's Stanley Park, Vancouver's largest urban park, a green oasis within the urban landscape, including 27 km of forest trails plus the 8.8 km seawall, a paradise for bike riders. And much more!

Austin, Texas

The 293-acre Walnut Creek Park contains 15 miles of shady trails, most of which are not particularly challenging but with a few steep sections, and several trails cross the creek. There's access by public transportation. One point of access, reachable by public transportation, is Zilker Park. This 13.8-mile Barton Creek Greenbelt features a waterfall. The River Place Nature Trail proves to outsiders that not all of central Texas is flat. There are steps to climb, ledges to carefully navigate, rapids crossed by hopping from one rock to another, and with an elevation gain of 548 meters / 1,800 feet. Some years ago, I was driven to Austin hikes but found no public transportation access to this one. Austin's public transportation has been expanding, so the hiker should check for the latest developments.

These are but a few of Austin's trails, best done in autumn, winter and spring. If you insist on summer, you might be moved to stop in a swimming hole and forget the hike. Unlikely in Austin to accumulate Everest points, but beautiful country within the city, nevertheless.

Philadelphia, Pennsylvania

The Wissahickon Valley Gorge has 57 miles (91.7 km) of trails, with thick forest, ruins of old mills, old stone bridges, historic plaques. With Philadelphia's excellent transit system, hikes are accessible via public transit. *USA Today* named the Schuylkill River Trail (accessible from downtown) as the "Best Urban Trail" in 2015. Great for cycling as well. Names like Pennypack Creek Trail, Manayunk Towpath and Forbidden Drive stimulate the hiker's imagination. Back in town, we find great historic walks as well as funky neighborhoods.

Paris

MOST PUBLIC STAIRWAYS

It is possible to accumulate Everest points by climbing public stairways. One urban hiker who wants to try this technique asked me how to calculate meters-climbed according to the number of steps on a stairway.

Here's my calculation. Each year they have a Chicago Willis Tower Stair Climb, called the SkyRise, to raise money for charities. The climb is 2,100 steps and the Tower (formerly Sears Tower) is 442 meters high. Divide 2100 steps by 442 meters and you come up with a rounded off figure of 4.7 steps per meter.

I've done my own measuring which makes it slightly more than 4.7 steps. Furthermore, not all steps are equal. To play it safe and not overestimate the number of meters climbed, I've decided to round it off to 5 steps per meter.

According to Doug Beyerlein, in his "uplifting" must-see site, PublicStairs.com, the USA rankings for the longest/highest urban staircases are as follows:

1. **Murphy Ranch East Stairway:** 512 stairs   Location: A park in east Los Angeles;

2. **Gil's Stairs:** 413 stairs Location: The Second Street Stairs stretch from West State Street to   MontelloAvenue in downtown Hood River, Oregon;

3. **56th Street Steps:** 394 stairs LocationPittsburgh, between Carnegie and Celandine streets;

4. **Howe Stairway:** 388 stairs Location: Howe Stairway runs under Interstate 5 in Seattle, from Franklin Avenue to 10th Avenue East;

5. **Filbert East Stairway:** 383 stairs Location: The Filbert East Stairway cuts through Pioneer Park in San Francisco.

Using 5 steps per meter, the Filbert East Stairway of 383 steps would be nearly 77 meters. When I run up the 250 steps to Sacré-Coeur in Montmartre, Paris, I'm climbing approximately 50 meters.

Leading U.S. cities in numbers of public staircases are Pittsburgh, Los Angeles, Seattle and San Francisco, in that order. The precise number of staircases depends on the counting method and different sources disagree. Paris, France, where I live most of the time, outdoes most American cities. It has 148 outdoor stairways, either as streets or connecting one street to another, but the municipality does not even include in this tally those staircases between lower and upper banks of the Seine, nor stairways within public parks, so a different tallying system might put Paris on top of Pittsburgh, which has 739 sets of public steps, because only 344 are legal streets.

Pittsburgh, Pennsylvania

Pittsburgh has done the most of any city to exploit its urban stepscapes. "Each October, the South Side Slopes Neighborhood Association sponsors the StepTrek, which offers two courses covering 2,500 of roughly 5,500 steps on the hillside. The patchwork of ascending trails meander by churches, small homes and mansions, through fields and along narrow alleyways, all providing breathtaking views of the Monongahela River and Downtown Pittsburgh. If you added up all of the elevation covered, according to the StepTrek website, you'd reach 1,460 feet — higher than the Empire State Building at 1,454 feet and the Eiffel Tower at 984 feet." (see *Pittsburgh, Insider's Guide*).

Pittsburgh also has a site called Wilderness in the City, Observatory Hill, 1,370 feet in altitude at its highest point, above the wooded trails of Riverside Park.

Can Pittsburgh qualify for Everest points? Ask Bill Fink (*https://www.southwestmag.com/stair-power/*): "The 739 outdoor stairways cover the city's hills with more than 45,000 individual steps, comprising 24,545 vertical feet in all—approaching a Mount Everest's worth of elevation. They're the single greatest assembly of outdoor public staircases in America, and perhaps the world."

That's 7,481 meters. Just do all of Pittsburgh's stair steps and you've surpassed an Everest!

Los Angeles, California

After Pittsburgh, Los Angeles has the most public staircases in the USA, with the highest step count of: 512 (see beginning of this chapter). On a clear day in the winter months from downtown, you can see the snow-covered San Gabriel Mountains in the distance. I once lived in a house reached by staircase in a neighborhood aptly named Highland Park, in the area where I   first discovered the network of staircases removed from major traffic arteries.

Consider the Music Box Loop, a vigorous walk built around the famous staircase in Silver Lake, one of a triplet of staircase communities that includes Highland Park and Echo Park. It was in Silver Lake where Laurel and Hardy made their 1932 academy award winning The Music Box, in which they were hired to deliver a piano ...up the stairs!

According to the indispensable website, *http://www.secretstairs-la.com/welcome.html*, "The staircases lace the hillsides of certain L.A. neighborhoods, and are historical reminders of a time when this was not a city of cars. City planners and developers installed them as direct routes for pedestrians—housewives and children particularly—to get down the hills to school,   the supermarket, and transit lines. The city at that time was well served by trolleys, streetcars, buses, and light-rail systems."

LA is also an urban climber's paradise. Just one of many examples: The Inspiration LoopTrail takes you from the Will Rogers home, just off Sunset Boulevard, past a polo field, and up a hill 202 meters / 662 feet, with   an expansive view from the top of the Pacific Ocean. Connecting with Will Rogers Park is the 67-mile Backbone Trail, officially opened in June 2016, with Metro bus connection.

The short hike up to the Griffith Park Observatory rises 177 meters / 512 feet, in one mile, with the reward at the top: a view of the city on one side and the San Fernando Valley on the other. In the same neighborhood, the 3-hour hike up to the Hollywood sign has an elevation gain of 335 meter / 1068 feet. Between Pasadena in the east and Pacific Palisades to the west are longer hikes with considerable gains in elevation.

Without any one huge mountain, the LA hiker will easily gain all the needed Everest points and more. Just do NOT light a match on the way through these often drought-affected forests. On a sad note, because of voracious real estate development, the LA tree canopy seems on its way to disappearing.

La Paz, Bolivia

But the two potential winners for sheer numbers of urban staircases are Hong Kong and La Paz, Bolivia. Both cities have countless urban public staircases, but La Paz may have the longest, and it definitely has the highest, since it's the highest capital city in the world. Hong Kong's Pound Lane, with its 238 steps, cannot compare with "The Thousand Steps" in La Paz, which is really "only" 916 steps.

In public stairways alone, hikers in La Paz can reach their Everest points, though other staircases with fewer steps are deemed safer for the urban explorer. La Paz's canyon geography allows for dozens of steep climbs within the city limits, including Devil's Tooth, which is capped by a monolithic rock. To get to the top, it's a steep 350-meter climb from the highway below.

Throughout the city, municipal authorities have designated a dozen viewpoints as Miradores. The climb to Killi Killi, towering over central La Paz, is at least 340 steps, plus several blocks of street climbing. Using the 5-steps-per-meter formula, my climb to the Killi Killi lookout is about 68 meters. So you can see that stair climbing, cumulatively, can lead to significant Everest points.

La Paz wins the competition for highest urban staircases, but that's just the starter. Its canyon landscape will please the multi-tasking urban hiker in every which way. And as we shall see in the next section, one can ride in public transportation beyond the La Paz city limits and reach peaks of 17,000 feet, with no technical equipment required.

Lisbon, Portugal

Lisbon gets an honorable mention in the realm of public staircases, not so much for their number but for how they integrate with the remarkable sidewalks, all mosaic. Yes, mosaic sidewalks are part of the overall colonial and Moorish architectural context. And this is the "city of seven hills" so there is so much aesthetic climbing with enriching panoramic views at the top: and below, the sea. Just be careful when it rains, as mosaic sidewalks can become slippery.

Cuzco, Peru

As with Lisbon, the sidewalks of Cuzco, Peru are integrated with the city's architecture. Before my stair-counting days, I walked the public street-stairs of Cuzco, many of them cobblestone. To your right and left, these stair-streets are lined with original Spanish colonial walls, amazingly built upon the Inca stone base! These public stairways are framed with precision Inca stonework. To this very day, no archaeologist is reasonably sure about how they moved and carved the huge boulders that would become earthquake-resistant walls.

The uphill climb from Cuzco, 3,400 meters / 11,155 feet to the impressive stone ruins of the Sacsayhuaman fortress is 300 meters in only 2 kilometers. The climb from Cuzco to Cristo Blanco, beginning in the San Blas neighborhood and then walking up, includes a 550-step staircase. This is 10 minutes above Sacsayhuaman.

There are many other hikes out of Cuzco, some a la carte and others requiring a tour agency. Cuzco could receive a Gold Medal were it not for the fact that it is overwhelmed with tourism. The trekking trail from Cuzco to Macchu Picchu is vulnerable to the adverse effects of overuse.

It's beyond the scope of this book to discuss the sustainability of mass tourism, nor do I have figures to say just how much the general population of Cuzco benefits economically from the industry. Like Montmartre in my Paris base camp, Cuzco retains its intrinsic beauty but earns a Silver rather than Gold Medal because of the sustainability issue.

La Paz: 916 steps

IDEAL ENDINGS: SPRAWL-FREE ACCESS TO WILDERNESS OR RURAL LANDSCAPES

The urban sprawl we find in wealthy countries has its equivalent with shantytowns in poor countries. Sprawl-Busters presents the case against sprawl from a perspective of wealthy countries.

"Sprawl" is defined by the National Trust for Historic Preservation as "poorly planned, low-density, auto-oriented development that spreads out from the center of communities. It creates that doughnut effect in some cities where acrylic and asphalt suburban shopping malls form a ring around the dead center, where the old downtown sits decaying."

The opposite phenomenon is no less demoralizing: the wealthy hold on to a gentrified urban enclave, driving up housing prices so the poor and middle classes are driven out. In Paris, where I live, social problems fester in highrise suburbs, and in Mexico City, where I lived some time ago, shantytowns surround much of the city.

Urban planners have attempted to apply a remedy called smart growth. It goes beyond the scope of Urban Everesting to evaluate the successes or failures of smart growth. I once taught university courses on smart growth but today I would not rehire myself. Smart growth can successfully contain a problem and offer temporary remedies, but I suspect that the deeper answer to our problems with sense of place and sense of space resides in some form of sustainable degrowth. That said, without hesitation I support smart growth advocates wherever I reside, since sprawling alternatives devastate our habitat.

Paradoxically, some of the greatest success stories in containing urban-suburban-peri-urban sprawl can be credited to geography itself.

New York City: The Long Path

Some of these Ideal urban endings are also the scene of the most glorious hiking opportunities. For example, thanks to the Hudson River, the hiker can walk out of Manhattan from beautiful Fort Tryon Park, across the Washington Bridge, the beginning of The Long Path. Today, The Long Path extends 358 miles from its official trailhead at the 175th Street Subway Station in Manhattan to John Boyd Thatcher State Park near Albany, connecting the most cosmopolitan area in the country with the region's wildest places. I've hiked both ends of the path on separate occasions, and long to do the whole route.

Marseille: Les Calanques

The city of Marseille in southern France hits its own happy ending thanks to this protected wilderness consisting of rugged high bluffs overlooking intimate coves of the Mediterranean. We got to the edge of the Calanques via city bus. The steep ups and downs between one rocky bluff and the next, as well as the descents into the pristine coves followed by the obligatory re-ascent involves enough climbing to earn some Everest points even though the base of the Calanques is at sea level.

The city of Marseille has designed a number of less challenging but aesthetic hikes within the city limits, as well as Grande Randonnée GR 2013, 365 kilometers around the perimeter of the geographically-challenging city. And one can also scale, a la carte, to Notre-Dame de la Garde church, 162 meters above the sea, with magnificent panoramas.

Auckland Coast to Coast Walk

Auckland has two ideal endings since it is located on an isthmus, New Zealand's narrowest neck of land. The 16 kilometer hike passes through five volcanic sites, through ethnically diverse territory containing 181 different ethnic groups and a wide variety of endemic flora and fauna. Mild climbing is involved, reaching 183 meters above harbor level. The Coast to Coast Walk is ranked by Lonely Planet as one of the top 10 city hikes, and in fact, the entire trail falls within city limits. A number of other hikes are accessible through public transport: bus or ferry, and you are not required to know the rules of rugby to hike in New Zealand.

Local Auckland newspapers have published recent stories on the threat of sprawl, with charged polemics. "The Government is being criticized for moving slowly in its efforts to remove Auckland's urban growth boundary— which, before the election, Labor suggested was crucial to fixing the city's housing crisis." Urban growth boundaries are a part of the smart growth program.

Some of New Zealand's best farmland lies just outside Auckland, so the tug-of-war between smart-growth urban containment and the need for more space to prevent sharp rises in housing costs will have to play itself out. None of the three cities mentioned has escaped the dilemmas of sprawl, but parts of these cities still have their ideal endings thanks to geographic barriers.

La Paz, one more time...

I've gone this route at least fifteen times. From the Villa Fátima neighborhood, northernmost side of La Paz, flag down any bus that says either Coróico or Caranavi, but ask the driver immediately, before you are seated, if he can let you off at La Cumbre. It's about a ¾ hour ride. Get off the bus at La Cumbre just before the highway begins to descend. You're at 4,600 m / 15,260 ft. It's a windy, stark mountain pass with jagged, snow-patched mountains on either side.

You have a choice of 300+ meter climbs on either side. To the right: a winding jeep track which leads to a relay station with a beautiful vertical view. I've seen tiny purple and yellow butterflies and an occasional alpaca herd along this trail. More interesting are the trails to the left, one leading to a peak Cerro Saturno (5,000 m) and another arriving at the most famous Inca Trail: Cumbre-Coroico, both with awesome 360-degree views. The safest season is the dry season between May and July.

I mention these climbs in the section because I recently discovered a way out of La Paz on foot, with a footpath that leads eventually to La Cumbre. I took it a few kilometers just to make sure it really got me out of the city, and then turned back before sundown, happy to have discovered another real ending in this city of canyons and gorges.

Paris

HIGH LINES

Paris, France

A revolution in urban walking began in Paris with the La Promenade Plantée in 1993. An urban walkway garden was built to replace an abandoned above-ground railroad track. Where the el ended and the track went below ground, the Promenade Plantée transformed into the Coulée Verte (Green Alley), beneath street level. This means that the stroller or long-distance urban walker can go 4.5 kilometers, from just east of La Bastille, central Paris, all the way to the edge of the city, reaching the immense Vincennes forest. Crossing through the forest, the walker who wants more arrives at the Bords de la Marne (Edge of the Marne River) pedestrian-and-cycling path, which leads all the way past the old-chic peri-urban city of Lagny, without having to confront any automotive traffic! This is a total of 30 kilometers of urban walking without more than two or three street lights.

New York City

The above-ground portion of the Promenade Plantée was the probable inspiration for a similar project in Manhattan on abandoned elevated train tracks: The High Line, with the ribbon-cutting ceremony for the opening of the final segment held in 2014. The High Line green way extends through several miles of extraordinary urban landscapes from the lower west side to around West 34th Street, mostly running parallel to 10th Avenue until a final loop. At this writing, there are plans to extend it. Like its Parisian ancestor, the High Line is accessed by stairways. Unlike its Paris counterpart, it does not connect with trails out of the city.

Seattle

The Burke-Gilman Trail in Seattle: an abandoned rail line that stretches from Seattle along Puget Sound to Redmond (Lake Sammamish), some 30 miles.

Paris

THE BEST CITIES FOR HIKING: RANKING

In order to compile these rankings, I've often relied on my own experiences, but when I've not hiked in a city, I've relied on eye-witness reports as well as in-depth research. I cannot claim that these rankings are purely "objective" but the innovation here is to have established measurable criteria to blend with subjective impressions. You can count altitude, you can count numbers of stairways and you can measure acreage of urban forests.

These criteria include: the Everest point system, the presence of large forests within city limits, the presence of outdoor public stairways, and urban "endings" that allow for quick access to either wilderness or rural landscapes. A fifth category has been added, the presence of "High Ways" which is beginning to trend.

Everest Points:
Enough challenging climbs to do 6,000 meters, with a double score if the city is at a high altitude or if it has numerous mountains from which to choose.

Large forest within city limits

Public staircases

Ideal Endings:
Places where the city ends and farmlands or the wild begin, with no sprawl transition

High Way Garden:
Promenades over abandoned rail tracks

Gold Medals
(alphabetical order, with best hiking seasons)

Cape Town, South Africa

(Average max of 27-29 Celsius between December and March may be too hot for some, since many of the climbs have no tree cover. Most precipitation in mid-winter, July-August, so be extra careful in those months when navigating slippery rocks.)

Grenoble, France

(Average maximum highs in the hot summer months are between 27 and 29 Celsius. The coldest months, December through February, are not hit with the extreme cold waves of a New York, Chicago or Boston, but be prepared for snow on trails in the winter. I've used snap-on crampons during mid-November hiking in the Alps.)

Hong Kong

(If you don't like hiking in 30 plus Celsius, the best months are November through April with increasing precipitation in April. Definitely avoid August monsoons.)

La Paz, Bolivia

(End of rainy season, April through September; never too hot, but sunblock is mandatory in thin air. Thanks to the altitude, no mosquitoes or other annoying creatures. Best times: before 11am and after 4pm for those bothered by the unfiltered sun.)

Los Angeles, California

(The nearer you get to the ocean, the more benign the weather. Rainy season in winter. Freshest months for hiking: March, April, May, June and November.)

Pittsburgh, Pennsylvania

(Least extremes in temperature April-May and September-October)

Portland, Oregon

(Benign temperatures year round but best to avoid long and incessant rainy season by hiking during the 7-month period between April and October.)

Quito, Ecuador

(Two rainy seasons: February, March and April, and then a short one in October. Year round maximum Celsius temperatures of between 13 and 14 degrees, mid-50s in Fahrenheit, practically require outdoor activity, just to keep warm. Cool eves perfect for sleeping.)

Rio de Janeiro

(Rio and Quito are both near the equator, but altitude is the determining factor that makes sea-level Rio so much hotter than mountainous Quito. May through October are the only 6 months where the average maximum temperature is less than 30 Celsius. June, July and August have the least precipitation: making the Southern Hemisphere winter the "coolest" hiking period.)

San Francisco, California

(In December and January, the average monthly high in Celsius hovers at only 14 degrees, 57F. Non-rainy season between mid-April and mid-October. Rarely ever too hot for a vigorous hike.)

Taipei, Taiwan

(Steamiest months in Taipei are between May and September, with November through March having the most benign hiking temperatures, with average-maximum high less than 24 Celsius: 75F. These are the months with the least precipitation as well.)

Vancouver, British Columbia, Canada

(Least precipitation plus warmest temperatures May through September.)

Silver Medals (in alphabetical order)

Auckland, New Zealand

(Average low in July-August winter is 8 Celsius and average high in January-February summer is 24 Celsius, so no bad months, though May through August gets 12-15 days of precipitation per month, and it's not a warm rain.)

Austin, Texas

(Summer months are only for the sturdiest hikers, though hiking trails often rescue the overheated hiker with swimming holes.)

Cuzco, Peru

(The average maximum high temperature year-round in Cuzco is between 20 and 22 Celsius, but it can feel quite hot under the midday unfiltered sun. Average maximum lows coldest June through August. There was no heating in the home of the family I stayed with and the technique at night is to bundle up under extra blankets.)

Lisbon, Portugal

(My wife and I hiked in and around Lisbon during a heat wave. Somehow a zesty strong Portuguese coffee before setting out on the trail made me well. Toughest months July through mid-September. The sweet nights make urban hiking a special treat, with superb views from high places.)

Marseille

(Calanques are sometimes closed in dry, hot summer months when forest fires threaten. Avoid July and August.)

New York City

(Typical US temperate weather, can be hot and humid in the summer and very cold in winter. No wonder the New York Marathon is run in early November.)

Paris, France

(But for an occasional extreme heat wave (canicule), Paris is neither too hot in the summer nor too cold in winter, though Parisians gripe about so many grey winter days. Average temperatures on the rise, according to old-timers who've been here their whole lives.)

Philadelphia, Pennsylvania

(Extremes of hot and cold make between seasons best for hiking, with near 30 Celsius average maximum highs June through August. Reports of deaths of divers and swimmers at Devil's Pool. Just too hot to resist the crystalline treated waste waters of the creek.)

Seattle, Washington

(Benign weather except for more rains between November and March.)

La Paz

SAFETY TIPS

For cities where potential crime is an issue, these simple and sensible tips published by the Cape Town Tourism Visitor Center, can apply.

- Avoid carrying large sums of cash, don't carry cameras in plain sight and do not leave belongings unattended.
- Heed the advice of your hosts or locals on where to go after dusk. Avoid walking in deserted and dark places at night.
- Never allow strangers to assist you in any way at ATMs or cash points. Street children and beggars may approach you for a handout. If you wish to help, consider giving food or donating to a registered charity.
- Keep copies of all valuable documents in a safe place. When exploring Table Mountain National Park, take a map, comfortable walking shoes, a few friends and a charged mobile phone.
- When hiking, be prepared for weather that can change rapidly, even in summer. Bring along enough water and sunblock, as well as something warm to wear. Start heading back well before dark and don't venture away from the demarcated paths. Tell a friend or your host where you are going and when you expect to be back.

ADDITIONAL CONCERNS, SAFETY AND OTHER

Stray dogs. In years of hiking in and around La Paz, as well as around other Latin American cities, I've never been bitten by a stray dog, but groups of strays can be frightening. I used to carry a stone, just in case, and that seemed to work, but a local farmer told me that carrying a stick is even more effective for dissuading the dogs.

Invisible walls. This dissertation has not been focused on tourism. I'm not one to rank the comparative merits of different cultures. However, the urban hiker will certainly want to visit places of interest in each city, getting there on two feet. Having written books on adjusting to life in foreign cities, I can affirm that the tourist industry often erects invisible walls around cores of cities, converting tourism into a type of Disneyland of culture, when in fact, some of the most appealing facets of life in a foreign city are found in neighborhoods beyond the tourist core. In Paris, where I have lived the longest, the tourist core significantly coincides with the former rampart that once circled the city.

Within this tourist enclave, places of business look at you as a transient, unlikely to ever return, so the shop or café owner has no legitimate self-interest in converting you into a regular customer, nor is he or she motivated to give you a fair price. There is much to be said in favor of the visitor spending time in regular neighborhoods beyond the tourist industry's demarcations.   In Paris, outer neighborhoods like Les Batignolles, La Butte aux Cailles and the east end districts are no less attractive, although funkier, than the streets around La Louvre.

Outside the core, the devoted walker will come upon one-way streets and alleyways in the 19th and 20th Arrondissements containing secret gardens and homespun street art, in surprisingly intimate settings. That's just an example.

Certainly, urban hikers are by nature explorers, and are well-rewarded by sauntering beyond the post-card districts of any city.

La Paz

CASE HISTORY: EVERESTING IN LA PAZ

Long before our attempt at earning an "Everest" in January of 2019, I may have qualified for the prize in Los Angeles County, but that was before I'd conjured up the urban everesting formula, and also prior to my serious logging of hikes and climbs.

On one Saturday, hiking with family, we made it to the top of Placerita Canyon, with a sprawling view of the gridded San Fernando Valley mouse maze. The elevation gain was 1,644 feet. At the top, I succumbed to the heat, took off my jacket, and hung it on a limb of a tree.

Once back to our home base, I realized I'd left the jacket at the top. Early on Sunday morning, I went back to Placerita, climbing to the top, wagering with myself on the probability of the jacket still being there. It was.

I thought it was a handsome jacket, but evidently, nobody wanted it.

The total feet climbed in those two consecutive days was 3,288 feet, already 16% of a 20,000-foot Everest award. No way to re-calculate all the hikes I did during that period, so I'll have to return to LA for a new and measurable try.

So now it was time to make amends in La Paz. For urban hikers and bike riders, the 3,600-meter / 12,000-foot altitude of the highest capital city in the world, with its rarefied air, makes it challenging enough to sit in an armchair. Just being sedentary at this altitude burns off calories.

This metropolis of a million inhabitants sits in a deep bowl between the high plane city of El Alto on one side and the Cordillera Real of the Andes on the other. Within what the locals call "The Hole" are rippling ravines carved out by dozens of rivers and underground streams.

My partner in this enterprise, my wife Martha Arraya, recalls walking to school as a child. There were a few flat streets but they never took her far. The norm consisted of climbs and descents, which she also dared to try on roller skates. She lives with me in a fourth-floor apartment just outside of

Paris, with no elevator, where she thinks nothing of climbing 60 steps with each return home, sometimes repeating the climb three or four times a day.

We also have a residence in La Paz, where we returned in 2019 to use as a base for some serious climbing, and we crafted a precision definition of the goal of everesting. We planned to climb an equivalent of what an Everest climber does from the Nepalese airport at Lukla, at 2,860 meters, to the base camp at 5,400 meters, and finally to the peak of Everest at 8,848 meters: rounded off to 6,000 meters, about 20,000 feet.

With such seductively disruptive topography in La Paz, we decided to everest mainly on foot, with cycling as a complementary medium, rarely repeating the same climbs, in order to enjoy the maximum number of the canyons, gorges and panoramic views, as well as discovering the varied socioeconomic geography within and around this rapidly integrating city categorized by the emergence of an indigenous "Aymara bourgeoisie."

Urban Stairways

In the USA, we've seen that the city with the most public stairways is Pittsburgh, with 739 sets of public steps, 344 of which are legal streets. There is no official count as to the number of public stairways in La Paz, but it exceeds a thousand. Not a thousand steps: a thousand stairways.

Our urban everesting project focused in part on the city's staircases, many of which reach lookouts (miradores) with awesome views of the city's colorful highrise architecture "competition" below, the theme-and-variations of canyons branching out from the two city centers, north and south, as well as the snow-covered peaks: Illimani (6,438 m), flat-topped Mururata (5,871 m) and Huayna Potosí (6,088m).

If we restricted all of our climbs to public staircases, we would need to climb nearly 30,000 stair-steps, with a 5-step-per-meter average multiplied by our 6,000-meter goal. We decided to blend the stairs with footpaths and some daunting street climbing as well, from the geographic base at Plaza Humboldt (3,250 meters) to the highest edges of the city at 4,000m. These hikes would add a transformative ingredient to our adventure, with so many trails passing abruptly from urbanization into rugged terrain and even wilderness, within municipal limits! La Paz tries to sprawl out, as if it were a North American city, but in many parts, the topography puts its foot down and says "No", and when developers insist on encroaching into the hillsides, Mother Nature, La Pachamama, sometimes can take no more, responding with violent landslides.

The most iconic of these in-your-face wilderness hikes is La Muela del Diablo (Devil's Tooth), a steep climb from the south zone whose peak is 3,825 meters, reachable on foot from our apartment nearly 500 meters below! When you get to the top, you decline into a green crater, a micro-climate where indigenous farmers and sheep herders reside far removed from the noise- and air-pollution of the streets of La Paz. But technically, they are still within the city limits, and can vote in the mayoral elections.

As seniors in our early 70s, we awarded ourselves a handicap, allowing for the fact that Everest climbers are going into thinner air than we have in La Paz. Nevertheless, even at our "lower" altitude, at an average 3,600 meters we take in 40% less oxygen per-breath than we breath in at the banks of the Seine.

Reality Touring

For our La Paz adventure we trained back in Paris on the city's 148 public stairways, well aware that public staircases go beyond fitness and serve as a direct route into understanding the complex workings of a society. We adapted our everesting mantra, legally plagiarized from former Paris mayor Bertrand Delanoe: "Anyone who wants to understand a city should take to its stairways, and those of Paris have often revealed the secrets of our city."

In La Paz we are looking at two distinct types of public staircases. For hill dwellers in the colder and higher sectors, stairways function as the streets that could not be built on such steep gradients. They connect mostly poorer residents with the nearest public transportation, much as did the many urban stairways in Los Angeles, California before the streetcar network was summarily dismantled.

In La Paz, many of these communities are encrusted precariously into the sides of what is essentially a canyon wall. When rural migrants could not afford rentals in lower districts, they created their own makeshift settlements, often using the cheapest red bricks, which gives hillsides in upper La Paz an earthy reddish hue. Looking up at this rugged collage, you can see the empty patches where Mother Earth, La Pachamama, defended herself with deadly landslides.

On the other hand, in more fashionable districts in the southern zone, people pay to have modernistic houses with a view, much like canyon dwellers in LA. The municipality affords these residents with vehicle access to their front gates via steep streets with hairpin turns. Stairways are implanted either for aesthetic reasons or to provide access to domestic employees when public transport drops them off below the hill.

The city of La Paz has made efforts to reduce the "stairway gap." Under the early direction of Ramiro Burgos, later director of mobility and transportation, the program Barrios de Verdad (Neighborhoods for Real) made cultural and infrastructural improvements in order to transition make-shift settlements into authentic neighborhoods. Part of this program, which has covered more than 100 neighborhoods, is to improve the public stairways, with safety railings and colorful paint.

I asked Mr. Burgos, if he could consider the staircases as a form of active public transportation. "I'm not sure I could go that far," he smiled warmly, "though for sure they play a vital role in connectivity."

A few La Paz residents warned us that some of these more isolated staircases might take us into no-go neighborhoods where some locals might be suspicious of strangers, wondering why anyone would want to appropriate their daily climbing obligation into leisure activity. Several locals warned us that stairways were a preferred hangout for thieves, alcoholics and drug addicts, since the police are too lazy to climb up on foot for a confrontation.

So we entered this adventure with circumspection.

Nevertheless, the city itself touts these stairways as part of its gritty charm and even features "The Thousand Steps" in its booklet, 50 Things You Should Do in La Paz, a stairway with 916 steps leading to El Alto. Legends from non-climbers said that outsiders entering the "Thousand Steps" would subject themselves to the risk of mugging and dog attacks.

Our strategy was to document each climb, whether by staircase, footpath or bicycle, with photos from bottom to top, and from top to bottom. In one of our first climbs, a neighborhood called Ventilla, we only shot photos at the entrance. As we got higher into the 87-step climb, the staircase came in direct, almost intimate contact with front doors to residences on either side, and we felt that taking photos would be an invasion of privacy. In an American city, "Neighborhood Watch" might have called the police on us.

On the opposite end of the spectrum is a steep hill that begins three blocks from our apartment, leading through the neighborhoods of El Porvenir and Las Kantutas, where the higher you go (140 steps in addition to considerable street climbing), the more extravagant the homes. Near the top was a guard post with a barrier that was only opened for known residents. Contrary to the Ventilla residents, in Las Kantutas, an automobile is indispensable. I wondered how good this could be for the environment if every time you forget to buy a loaf of bread or tube of toothpaste, you have to turn on your engine, drive down a hairpin street to the Ketal supermarket and then drive back up to a 150-meter perch.

Or, from an optimist's point of view, how superb it could be for your health if you regularly forgot to buy something at the market and on a daily basis did the descent plus climb on foot. I considered the ultimate redundancy: building an exercise gym at the top of the hill and driving up to get there.

Within the densely populated hole of La Paz, air quality is questionable, but in both the poorer and wealthier neighborhoods with a view, stairways isolated from through traffic provide notable breathing relief.

Obstacles

After the first week it became apparent that climbing 6,000 meters in 30 days was not as easy as simply walking up stairs. As the youngest of her generation, Martha had family caretaking duties and out of solidarity I would accompany her. We did the best to find climbing near her visits with family. She agreed to support me on as many climbs as possible, camera in hand, leaving the complete Everesting goal to me.

She'd be happy with a partial everest, knowing that the climbing itself was not a physical obstacle and that family solidarity should not be sacrificed.

Even without the family duties, public transport between one climb and another was time-consuming. Dental appointments also interfered. If we'd had tooth problems on the real Everest, even the shrewdest of Sherpas would not be able to find a dentist for us.

Nor could some slow time spent with friends at some of La Paz's quirky new cafés be compromised. Urban everesting is, after all, supposed to allow for normal human relations to survive, between hiking segments.

Martha and I were good partners but we were not in it for identical purposes. She wanted to showcase her exciting city and found certain climbs too coarse to be called attractive. Aesthetics was more important to her than the competitive milestone of 6,000 meters. She grew up in La Paz with friendships based on longstanding companionship, and in fact, her group of school friends continue to hold get-togethers some 50 years after their shared schooling.

For me, growing up in New York was very much a competitive venture. We gambled on everything, from baseball cards to basketball free throws. I've tried to minimize this competitiveness by studying Buddhist and Tarahumara histories, but I recognize that my essential competitive foundation simmers beneath the surface. I thrived on an Everest goal.

After the first five days, with less than 2,000 steps climbed, I decided to launch into morning bike climbs, for the pleasure, for sure, but also to accumulate a reserve of altitude meters, just in case the foot climbing should fall short. Martha approved, but warned me that La Paz drivers owned the roads and had no mercy for bicycle encroachers.

Some of the stair climbs did not fall neatly into the poor vs. affluent categories. From the Kantutani highway spiraling deep into "The Hole," we needed to scale to the Sopocachi neighborhood around Plaza España, in what could be labeled "the groin of the city." In this Sopocachi Bajo quadrant, the terrain is so convoluted that few streets can make it through. This was essentially a middle class neighborhood but with the access challenges of poorer sectors.

In fact, Sopocachi Bajo is one of 20 neighborhoods designated as "poorly served by public transport," according to a report by one of Bolivia's major newspapers, La Razón ("Lack of Public Transport Affects Residents of at Least 20 Neighborhoods," 6 September 2015). The city responded by expanding the Pumakatari public bus system, whose specialty is to reach poorly served neighborhoods where privatized mini-buses find it unprofitable to venture. But so far, no Pumakatari in Sopocachi Bajo.

For us to climb from the Kantutani highway to Plaza España, it took 439 steps in 7 separate staircases. We ended at the Montículo lookout, with a view of Illimani, shrouded, on this sunny day, on what appeared to be its own personal cloud, manufactured by its stunning but endangered glaciers.

Lookouts

Some of the higher climbs lead to belvederes that the city calls Miradores. Stairways to the lookouts pass through neighborhoods, but they have a second function: an outing for students of living history. Municipal pamphlets recommend buses or minibuses that climb laboriously through hairpin turns in order to arrive at the entrance of lookouts, but we located hidden pedestrian points of access.

Such was the case for Killi Killi, a steep hill located between downtown and the Miraflores neighborhood. Killi Killi was once a strategic point for the indigenous Aymara population to lay siege upon the city during wars of independence against the Spanish and Criole occupiers. We discovered the secluded foot entrance on a dead-end street, two blocks north of Plaza Uyuni, at 3,600 meters above sea level. In all there were 343 steps to the top, alternating with non-stair footpaths and a few blocks of street climbing as well. The total elevation gain was 118 meters, with the lookout at 3718m above sea level.

As with most of our stair climbs, the total meters scaled blended stair steps with footpaths or streets. In the case of Killi Killi, 68 meters were accounted for by stairways and the 50 remaining meters by street and path climbing.

La Paz

Lookouts are advertised by the city for sightseeing but our method involved "sight doing." Strangely, if you consider the time spent waiting for the bus, followed by the elongated trip with stops along the way over tight curves, walking up seemed like the practical option.

Our mirador goal was to scale at least ten of the official ones, while planning on discovering our own personal miradores that had not been officially designated as such.

Climbing Strategy

One of the major enemies for urban hikers in La Paz is the unfiltered sun. For us, sunblock is indispensable, but even then, it is best to avoid doing battle with the sun between 11am and 4pm, unless you choose one of the few wooded trails, such as the 200 meter climb from urbanized Irpavi II neighborhood, through a dense Eucalyptus forest (soothing for my asthma) to the agricultural and dairy village of Chicani. (Yes, Chicani remains a rural village, but it is situated within the municipal boundaries!) Along the way up to Chicani, it is common see and hear the gurgling natural springs, coming out of the ground right at our feet.

In Chicani the classic struggle against urban sprawl is taking place. The land is valuable and real estate developers want it. The villagers have banded together into a tight clan, in defense of their benign micro-climate, and thus far they've resisted. One of the factors that gives a city positive points for urban hiking is the possibility to make it on foot from an urbanized environment to rural agriculture, without having to pass through suburban sprawl. The Chicani climb, which begins at the Psychiatric Hospital at the upper edge of Irpavi, is an ideal example.

Following hairpin turns through a eucalyptus forest, with views of the Andean foot-mountains in the background, and in the foreground, a lucky few Swiss chalet dwellers, we reached the last leg of the climb, one of the few Main Streets in the world lined with dairy farms. Our elevation gain was nearly 300 meters.

With the scarcity of wooded climbs like that of Chicani, those urban climbers with sun problems need to choose that particular time of day when the mountains and gorges do best at shielding from the sun. In the case of the new lookout/ecological park called Auquisamaña (south zone), after 4pm, the hills offer shelter.

The climb begins at the end of the 21st Street neighborhood called San Miguel, La Paz's unofficial downtown of café culture. Before climbing, we can stop in a funky café and dope up with an artisanal blend of authentic Bolivian coffee.

Once you cross the river, you begin climbing through the beautiful residential neighborhood of Auquisamaña. Red and purple bougainvillea broadcast the elegance of colonial residences, with some of these homes backed up right against the canyon wall.

Normally the Pachamama strikes with landslides in poorer neighborhoods but in February of 2017, a hill came crashing down in Auquisamaña, spraying thick dust into the air and totally burying at least one home. Fortunately, no one was inside when it happened. In my archives from a previous saunter, I have the "before" pictures of those ill-fated homes.

Eventually the housing ends and a cobblestone road winds up through the steep hills. Supposedly we were headed for a new park-mirador, but from below we could see nothing above but a road disappearing on a hairpin. We'd lost a half hour waiting out a rainstorm.

In our partnership, Martha is the prudent one, you could call her a skeptic, while even at 73 years of age, I suffered from vestiges of adolescent brashness. At one point, we needed to descend down a narrow ledge/path skirting a wall that led to the road. At the end of the path was a tool shed, and Martha suspected the presence of guard dogs. I did a reconnaissance mission, reaching the tool shed …no barking, and then went back up to get her, like a true "caballero."

Her greater concern was about our having to return in the dark. Since the supposed lookout could not be seen from the road below, Martha feared a long climb that would leave us descending after sundown. So I did another reconnaissance climb, and it turned out the lookout was right around the bend, and included a cozy pine forest, not visible from Martha's viewpoint.

I descended, like a gallant gentleman, in order to accompany my partner back up to the lookout. Within the forest there were shady trails which we scaled, deeper into the rough mountainside. We resolved to arrive earlier on another day with sandwiches and chocolate bars, in order to do leisure walks through these trails and then have our picnic with the expansive view of the former sheep-raising village of Ovejuyo, the mysterious cavernous Valley of the Spirits, the brashly colorful South Zone directly below, rippling canyons straight beyond the urbanization, and the hole of downtown La Paz in the distance, which thanks to our nearly 300-meter gain in altitude, was no longer above us.

It's an understatement to declare that this view is spectacular. I seriously considered becoming a hermit and staying up here under one of the wooden-roof shelters, with only occasional forays down the canyon slope to secure provisions.

According to my city-of-La Paz contour map, the total climb was 250 meters, equivalent to 1,250 stair steps, with another 50 meters on our street-climbing approach to the trailhead. At this point in our accumulation of everest points, 10 days into our expedition, we could do this climb 15 more times and reach our Everest. But we'd agree to only repeat a climb for a valid aesthetic reason.

Many of the other climbs I'd mapped out were questioned by my pragmatic partner. I became exasperated when she wished to veto certain climbs. Twenty years earlier, I'd gotten lost in the Cordillera at 5,000 meters, when a sudden fog swept in, so thick that I could barely see my own shoes. Like the ill-fated Christopher McCandless, in Into the Wild, I had been brashly overconfident. I did not even carry a pocket compass, since I felt I knew the terrain like my own backyard. Nor did I carry extra food or layers of clothing in case I'd be forced to stay overnight.

Paris

I'd lost my bearings for 7 endless hours (a great way to expand psychological time) with no llama turds on the ground to assure the presence of shepherds. I'd already made two exhausting climbs when a brief opening in the sky exposed a third climb that I'd have to make to get out to the highway. I could only do five steps at a time before resting on a rock, exposed to battering humid winds. The extra sweater Martha had suggested I take would have eased the agony.

I mention this because each time Martha now proposed to veto a climb for this or that danger, I knew she could at any time trot out the fact that I had nearly died of hypothermia in the mountains for not having taken her advice.

With certain climbs excluded from our menu, even ones I'd done before, I feared not reaching the 6,000 meters within the 30 allotted days. When our final week arrived, following a series of family crises and dental visits, we were still short of the 6,000 meters by 1,300!

A Call for Divine Intervention

The model for the Plurinational State of Bolivia is to consider language and cultural groups as "nations." The Aymara nation is centered in the La Paz region.

Ostensibly a Catholic country, the religion practiced by many Bolivians is a syncretic blend of Catholicism and indigenous faiths. Take a look at the facade of the colonial cathedral, San Francisco, in downtown La Paz, and you will see mestizo images on the surface. That said, more traditional Catholic culture still exists in parts of Bolivia.

Needing to make up 1,300 climbing meters within a week, we set out to do two Catholic pilgrimage climbs. The first of these Calvarios was Schoenstatt, in the south zone of the city. Located in a wooded sanctuary, with a chapel below and a huge white cross above, Schoenstatt is an Apostolic movement that began in Germany.

The climb to the cross consists of 14 hairpin turns, each stage with a white cross at the end. Once I completed the relatively short climb, I descended and asked the receptionist in the welcoming building whether people are known to do this climb twice.

"Not that I know of," she said.

I figured that if divine intervention were to help us reach the 6,000 meters, I'd have to do the climb a second time in order to gain an advantage over the other pilgrims: my New Yorker psychology. So I repeated the climb. Altogether, counting the elevation gain from our apartment to the Schoenstatt trailhead, I'd gained 230 meters. Not enough to make a dent.

Martha was waiting for me at her sister's house. We'd decided that two pilgrimage routes the same day would increase the chance for divine intervention on our behalf, so after lunch with the family, we decided to do a more challenging pilgrimage, aptly named Mirador El Calvario, in the northern sector of the city.

At the top was the oldest Mirador in La Paz, a pilgrimage sanctuary chapel with views of the lower city (left) and various parts of the rugged central La Paz urban geography straight ahead and to the right. The 220-meter ascent included rustic staircases, secluded working class neighborhoods, and some of the steepest streets in the city, ending with hairpin turns which, as with Schoenstatt, had crosses at the end of each turn.

For the day, we'd gained 450 meters in elevation, putting us in a position to achieve the Everest.

More biking, stopping to climb every hill along the way, we came upon our last good day for climbing, deciding to confront the 916 steps that lead to the Yellow Line Teleférico station in El Alto, at 4,000 meters above sea level. None of the stray dogs considered us intruders, and the muggers supposedly lurking on this staircase never showed up.

Dodging rain clouds, we did it, celebrating with fried chicken and espresso coffee in the panoramic restaurant above the Teleférico station, taking in an expansive view that included many of the climbs we had done during the month. We could see the path to Chicani, the hillside forest of Auquisamaña, and both Calvarios we'd done the day before.

All in all, I'd scaled 20,000 feet / 6,100 meters, with Martha having done at least 4,500 meters. This total includes 7,233 stair steps, with 1,145 meters (17+% of the total) climbed by bicycle.

I saw this as a beginning. Los Angeles, California was doable. We bought tickets for Portland, Oregon. And why not Hong Kong or Taipei?

With the potential air travel for the folks addicted to urban everesting, environmentalists could question our ecological footprint. This is a serious issue, what with the endangered melting glaciers around my beloved La Paz.

I hereby appear before the Court of Environmental Justice. We have no car, walk or bike to our home-city engagements, and live in a small apartment with no air conditioning. We do not eat red meat, and we are meticulous recyclers. Air travel to an urban everesting is our only carbon-footprint luxury, and we do so mainly to places where we have family responsibilities.

Surely my air travel to visit children or grandchildren should not get the same negative carbon points as that of a person who takes an airplane to Puerto Vallarta for a weekend vacation, stays in an air-conditioned hotel, and then rents a car.

I suppose that the ultimate philosophical point of Urban Everesting is that it can be done locally, in the city where you live. This leaves us with one unanswered question...

San Francisco

WHAT IF I LIVE IN A FLAT CITY?

Before we get accused of geographic discrimination, there's an answer for folks in flat cities like Chicago, London and Copenhagen. According to *azcentral.com*, part of the *USA Today* network, "You will burn 2 to 3 times more calories climbing stairs at a slow pace than walking briskly on level ground (see, Patti Davis, "Stairs vs. Walking for Cardio").

I'm not sure I understand the math, and I've seen contradictory equivalents on physics and sports medicine websites. But just for argument's sake, in order to equal a given amount of stair climbing, you'd have to walk, briskly, for three times as long as you would spend climbing. It took me an hour and 15 minutes to climb the steepest Placerita Canyon trail in Los Angeles County, Santa Clarita, with a gain of 1,644 feet in altitude.

The walker in Chicago would have to do about 3 hours and 45 minutes to equal the burnt calories. That's the distance along the Lake Michigan beachfront from Hide Park on the south side, where I once lived, to Lincoln Park, near north.

The problem is aesthetics. If the flat hike is dull, then it's not sustainable. But the beachfront of Lake Michigan, with its skyline views, is an attractive proposition. Furthermore, Chicago has a number of authentic old neighborhoods, where walking is a sensorial pleasure.

When my bike was stolen in Paris, before finding a replacement, I did my commutes on foot, more than doubling my commute time. But taking much longer to walk was better for me than being subjected to the sensorially dead underground non-place of the Paris Metro.

There must be some reasonably scientific formula to find the time/distance flat-walking equivalent of a stair climb or ascent of an urban mountain. Urban everesting most surely has an equivalent in a flat city, but with neither a bio-medical background nor competence in the fluid mechanics realm of physics, the calculation of Everest points in flat geography is best left to your personal physician and your personal physicist.

The complexity of the calculation for Chicago, the Windy City, involves the energy output in hiking against the wind, as well as hiking on the Lake Michigan beachfront sands. Who knows, hiking in deep sands against the wind might be more strenuous than going up stairs. If tomorrow I were thrust into an apartment in a flat city and had to stay there, I would relish the opportunity to create my own everesting formula.

Prague

San Francisco. Your dog will love urban everesting!

Made in the USA
Columbia, SC
27 November 2020

25700540R00039